Baby Girl's Holiday

Written By: Shaniqua Iran Harris
Illustrated By: Orlando Walker

Published by Gift From Above Publishing, LLC
www.giftfromabovepublishing.org
PO Box 1856
Rincon, GA 31326
ISBN: 978-0578-33841-5

Cover Design by: Orlando Walker
Illustrated by: Orlando Walker

Printed in USA

Message to the Readers

To all Daddy's girls who now have Angels, remember that love lives on through absence. May our dads continue to watch over, guide, and protect us always!

Dedication Page

For one more moment with you, there is nothing I would not give. I choose to honor your life by sharing my memories of the impression of love you left on my life. Edward Delmar Grant, you were an extraordinary father. I will always be your "BabyGirl," and you are forever my Angel.

~Shaniqua

Special Thanks to my children Milaiza Kelly (BabyGirl the Remix) and Jelani Harris; Being your mother has been my life's greatest accomplishment. Continue to live out loud and follow your dreams.

Thank you to my support system of family & friends who continuously encourage and motivate me.

Nakia & Kedere – Thank you for always supporting any and every dream that lies within me.

Nicole- you inspired and pushed me to complete this project when I thought it was impossible.

Natasha- my sister, friend, a partner in crime turned spiritual sister- your belief in me is unmatched!

R.P.- "You brighten my days." Thank you for keeping me grounded and allowing me to be an open book with you.

Q – The way you hold me accountable for my goals is something I will forever treasure. "You make me better."

To my FDA family, I thank you for loving all of me!

Orlando Walker- my brother, my AMAZING Illustrator! My work becomes magic when you Bless it with your talent.

Lastly, my brothers Kinsley and Curtis, the love and support you two have shown me this year, has pushed me beyond my limits.

I thank you all! I love you all!

- Shaniqua AKA BabyGirl

Out of a plastic bag, I pulled my pink and purple cabbage patch kid nightgown and slippers.

Tears began to roll down my smiling face as I remembered...

Spicy greens and sweet cornbread smothered the air. The melody of The Temptations melted my heart. Blue, Melvin. Otis, Paul, and Eddie harmonized in the background, enchanting my spirit.

Clap…2…3, Step…2…3, hand to waist, front –
and slide… I muttered in my head as I danced.
I had momentarily become one of The
Temptations.

Reminiscing how I inherited my love of the group
from my dad, my smile overflowed with joy. The
two of us danced, smiled, and shared our happiness.
Our bond was inseparable.

Although it was the eve of Thanksgiving, we loudly and proudly sang "Come They Told Me – Ba Rump A Bum Bum!" I closed my eyes, singing into the big silver cooking spoon and marching behind my dad, following his every footstep.

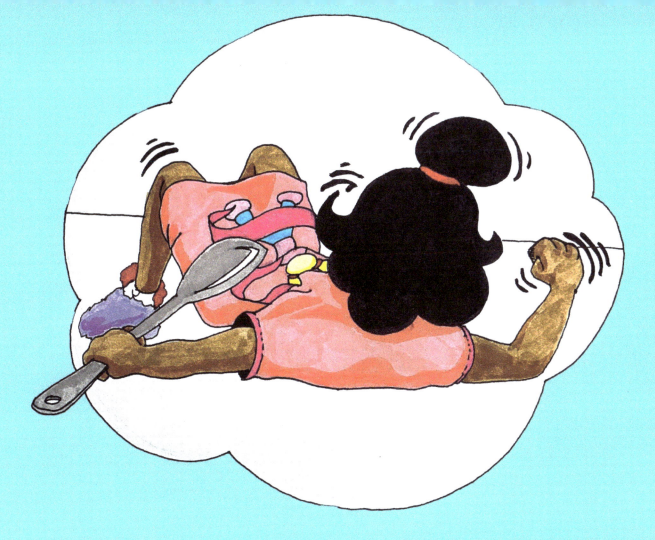

Caught up in the moment, singing, marching, and twirling around, then Ba Boomp! was the next sound heard as my little body crashed to the ground.

My dad rushed to my rescue like a knight in shining armor!

"It's alright, BabyGirl!" he said, while he held me in his arms and brushed off my knee. Although it still hurt, I knew I would be ok because my dad said so.

mmediately, I began to grin while hugging my dad and jumping back into action.

Childishly screeching, "Hang on the mistletoe, I'm gonna get to know you better-This Christmas.

And as we trim the tree, how much fun it's gonna be together-This Christmas. Fireside is blazing bright, and we're caroling through the nighttttt! And this Christmas will be-a very special Christmas for youuuuu and Me!"

My purple cabbage kid slippers were sliding and twisting while my little fingers snapped on the one hand. With the other, I maneuvered my cooking spoon microphone.

My dad had stopped singing and was watching in awe of how my young mind had grown to love the same music he loved.

As the song wound down, I slid over to the brown wooden cabinet door and tapped my dad on the leg. I innocently looked up at him and begged for a spoon of sweet potato pie mix.

We giggled as he snuck me the spoon before my mom came back into the kitchen. I laughed and licked the spoon with a pure appreciation for the sweet delight that danced on my tongue.

My dad looked on with kind, loving eyes, and I knew that
he approved of my joy. It wasn't enough to ruin my
appetite for dinner but just enough to give me another
moment of happiness.

Excitedly I asked, "Can we go in the living room?"
"Let's Go!" said my dad.

We put the big cooking spoon in the sink. As we were getting ready to walk, I shouted, "Let's March!". Happily we marched to the tunes of my imaginary drums.

Overwhelmed with excitement, I jumped up and down at the sight of the living room. It was purely magical!

There were warm, colorful lights on the large, fat green Christmas Tree. Stockings were hanging all around the room. Shiny red apples and bright, juicy oranges sat on the tables in the beautiful glass bowls that we couldn't touch.

There were walnuts, almonds, and macadamia nuts sprinkled around the fruit. Colorful hard candy filled th candy dishes. Candy canes were dripping from the tree and the room was overflowing with presents!

I knew not to touch anything, but the sight was enougl to brighten my world.

As I began to ask a question about Santa, my dad turned up the volume on the music. "Love comes with Christmas and goes with every other day of the year," I sang loudly into the air.
We looked at each other and smiled as we kept singing.

Filled with the aromas of spicy greens, sweet cornbread, stuffing, savory turkey, macaroni & cheese, sweet potato pies, coconut cake, The Temptations, my dad and I, the air in my world was an immeasurable amount of love & happiness!

When I close my eyes and listen to The Temptations "Give Love At Christmas" album, I can see my dad's face. I can hear his hearty laugh and feel the irreplaceable love and light he brought to my life.

If I had one wish to make, I'd wish to turn back the hands of time to the Holidays.

About the Author

Shaniqua Harris is a native of the Brownsville, Brooklyn section of New York. She has been an educator with the New York City Department of Education for 14 years. Shaniqua loves children, writing, butterflies, and giraffes. She adores the colors brown and purple. She enjoys making others happy through her writing. Shaniqua plans to continue writing children's books and bringing joy to the world through the eyes of BabyGirl.

Photo Credit: Lanii's Lens
(Jelani Harris)